Collins

Cherry Blossoms

Rhymes and Stories

LKG

FS2

SERIES EDITOR: RANI THIPPAVAZZULA

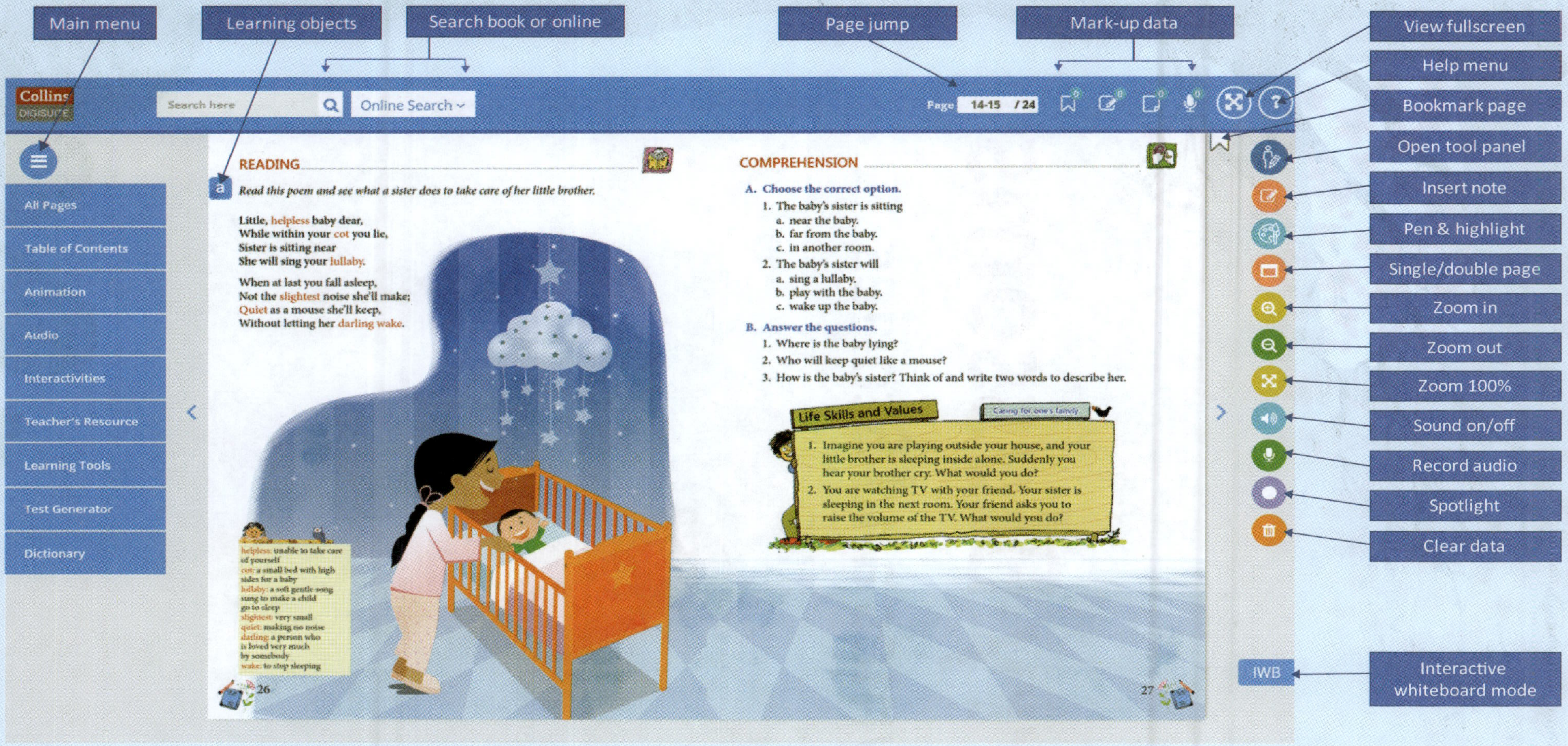

Student + Teacher			Teacher-only	
a animations	ia activities	g games	lp lesson plans	tn teacher's notes
ilt instructor-led tutorials	w worksheets	v videos	w worksheets	ak answer keys
	audio			

Preface

Cherry Blossoms provides graded, age-appropriate learning opportunities targeting holistic skill development for children in the age group of 3 years to 8 years. The series aligns with the vision outlined in the National Education Policy, 2020 for early years. It spreads across five levels, Nursery (Foundational Stage 1) to Class 2 (Foundational Stage 5). The books use a combination of hands-on activities, frequent recapitulation and child-friendly artwork to facilitate learning.

The series comprises **40 books** and spans **English**, **Maths**, **General Awareness**, and **Art and Craft**. The series comes bundled with a **workbook** for each subject and a book of **rhymes** and **stories** for Foundational Stage 1 to 3.

This series integrates the essence of **NIPUN Bharat** guidelines, which extensively deal with Foundational Literacy and Numeracy. The series aims to motivate learners to read independently, to improve their vocabulary, number sense and spatial understanding. The **Foundational Literacy and Numeracy (FLN)** skills include the skills for developing their critical thinking, logical reasoning and creative skills, as well as the skills to enhance their ability to express themselves both verbally and in writing.

Cherry Blossoms Teacher Support Materials include:

Teacher's Resource Books: Comprises stories, activity banks, classroom management and assessment guidelines

Multimedia eBook: Consists of animations, audio, video, slide shows, and interactive exercises

Print-ready Worksheets: Additional worksheets for practice and reinforcement, present in the digital support

Digital Flashcards: Flashcards with embedded sounds and animations for letter formation and letter-sound association

Animations and Songs: Animated stories and rhymes set to tune

Interactive Games: Interactivities to reinforce concepts in a fun and engaging manner

A note on the activity banks (included in the Teacher's Manuals)

The activity banks comprise hands-on activities that will help children develop the requisite skills to attain age-appropriate learning goals. In keeping with Howard Gardener's theory of multiple intelligences, the activity banks include options and variations that enable teachers to provide a planned cycle of experiences and opportunities, which foster each type of intelligence, to every child in their classrooms. The activity banks equip teachers to use the strengths of children as a means of complementing their less developed areas by valuing and nurturing the inherent abilities of the children.

Rani Thippavazzula, former Academic Director, Ravindra Bharathi Group is an eminent educationist with over two decades of experience in teaching, administration and curriculum design and development. As an Academic Advisor for chain schools pan India, she is proficient in developing learning products and is a specialist in Differentiated Instruction, Enterprise Education and Early Childhood Education.

Learning and Development During the Early Years

The early years are the most significant years for growth, development and learning. During this period, children need adequate opportunities for stimulating experiences as these favourably affect various learning abilities. Learning experiences, when chosen and planned properly, fuel the innate curiosity of children, and stimulate their thought processes.

The goal of learning during the early years is to enhance the all-round development of personality and to inculcate healthy attitudes, life skills and good values. Creative play, well thought-out games and developmentally appropriate activities help children develop the necessary skills to achieve these goals. The skills that children need to acquire can broadly be categorized as:

Motor:
Motor skills pertain not only to gross motor activities like walking and jumping but also include fine motor activities like the ability to hold a pencil and write. The development of motor skills is facilitated through several graded activities.

Personal, Social and Emotional:
Personal, social and emotional development, necessary for the overall personality development of children, is achieved using a combination of hands-on activities, role plays and thought-provoking stories and rhymes.

Linguistic:
The ability to listen, speak, read and write is critical to success in formal learning environments.

Mathematical:
The development of mathematical ideas and concepts is important at this stage since children will continue to build on this learning for most of their years of schooling.

Knowledge and Understanding of the World:
This is achieved through activities that enable children to explore their surroundings at home and in the school, and interact with the people that they see around them.

Health and Safety: The idea of health and safety is introduced through activities, stories and retelling of real-life experiences to encourage children to focus on health and well-being.

Creative:
Creative skills are developed through a host of activities involving art, craft, painting, roleplays, etc.

Logical and Rational Thinking:
Activities that involve simple puzzles, pattern-completion and visual discrimination help children to develop logical and rational thinking skills.

Contents

MY UMBRELLA GOES UP

My umbrella goes up
When the rain falls down,
When the rain falls down on me.
My umbrella goes up
When the weather's wet,
To keep the rain off me!

PAT-A-CAKE

Pat-a-cake, pat-a-cake,
Baker's man,
Bake me a cake,
As fast as you can.

Prick and pat it,
And mark it with T,
And put it in the oven
For teacher and me.

THERE'S A WORM IN THE GARDEN

There's a worm in the garden,
And his name is Wiggly Woo.
There's a worm in the garden,
And all that he can do,
Is wiggle all night,
And wiggle all day,
Whatever else the people say.
There's a worm in the garden,
And his name is Wiggly Woo.

THE LITTLE BIRD

Once I saw a little bird
Come hop, hop, hop.
So I cried, "Little bird,
Will you stop, stop, stop?"

And I was going to the window,
To say, "How do you do?"
But he shook his little tail,
And far away he flew.

HERE WE GO ROUND THE MULBERRY BUSH

Here we go round the mulberry bush,
The mulberry bush, the mulberry bush.
Here we go round the mulberry bush
On a cold and frosty morning.

This is the way we wash our face,
Wash our face, wash our face.
This is the way we wash our face
On a cold and frosty morning.

This is the way we comb our hair,
Comb our hair, comb our hair.
This is the way we comb our hair
On a cold and frosty morning.

This is the way we brush our teeth,
Brush our teeth, brush our teeth.
This is the way we brush our teeth
On a cold and frosty morning.

This is the way we put on our clothes,
Put on our clothes, put on our clothes.
This is the way we put on our clothes
On a cold and frosty morning.

MARY HAD A LITTLE LAMB

Mary had a little lamb,
Its fleece was white as snow;
And everywhere that Mary went,
The lamb was sure to go.

O-B-E-Y

O-B-E-Y
Obey your Mom and Dad.
O-B-E-Y
Makes them really glad.
Listen to the words they say.
Obey your parents every day.
O-B-E-Y
Obey your Mom and Dad.

SIX LITTLE DUCKS

Six little ducks that I once knew,
Fat ones, skinny ones, fair ones too.
But the only little duck with
Feathers on his back,
He led the others with a
'Quack, quack, quack!'

LITTLE BO-PEEP

Little Bo-Peep has lost her sheep,
And doesn't know where to find them.
Leave them alone and they'll come home,
Wagging their tails behind them.

MY LITTLE PUP

My little pup can jump up high.
He chases his tail,
I don't know why.
He loves to fetch the ball I throw,
It's fun to see how quick he grows.

I HEAR THUNDER!

I hear thunder,
I hear thunder!
Oh! don't you? Oh! don't you?
Pitter, patter raindrops,
Pitter, patter raindrops,
I'm wet through,
I'm wet through!

ONE, TWO, THREE, FOUR, FIVE

One, two, three, four, five,
Once I caught a fish alive.
Six, seven, eight, nine, ten,
Then I let it go again.
Why did you let it go?
Because it bit my finger so.
Which finger did it bite?
This little finger on the right.

THE LITTLE FINGERS

I have ten little fingers and ten little toes,
Two little arms and one
little nose,

One little mouth and two little ears,
Two little eyes for smiles
and tears,
One little head and two
little feet,
One little chin;
That's ME, complete!

ONE, TWO, BUCKLE MY SHOE

One, two,
Buckle my shoe.

Three, four,
Knock at the door.

Five, six,
Pick up sticks.

Seven, eight,
Lay them straight.

Nine, ten,
A big, fat hen.

Eleven, twelve,
Dig and delve.

Thirteen, fourteen,
Maids a-courting.

Fifteen, sixteen,
Maids in the kitchen.

Seventeen, eighteen,
Maids in waiting.

Nineteen, twenty,
My plate is empty.

THE FISH LIVES IN THE BROOK

The fish lives in the brook,
The bird lives in the tree,
But home is the nicest place,
For a little girl like me.

RINNI'S TOYS

Rinni is a big girl.
She goes to school every day.
She comes back home and
plays on her mother's computer.

One day, Rinni got a letter.
Rinni did not know who
sent the letter to her.

She opened the letter and read it.

Dear Rinni,
We are your toys. You have forgotten us. We are very sad. Do you remember how much you liked to play with us? Rinku didi wanted to throw us away. But mother saved us. Don't you love us anymore? We miss you Rinni!
Lots of love,
Your sad toys

After reading the letter, Rinni became sad.

She got out all her toys. She played with them and shared them with her sister.
Now, Rinni, her toys and sister play happily!

RAJU'S KITE

I am Raju's kite.
I live in the cupboard with his bat and ball.
I am blue but my tail is red and yellow.

Last Sunday, Raju took me to the terrace.

There was a gentle breeze.
I flew up high in the sky.
I was so happy!
I danced with joy in the cool breeze.
Soon, a big white kite came next to me.
We danced together.
We had a lovely time!

Sadly, our tails got tangled while we were dancing. Raju kept pulling at my string. I tried to free my tail.

Suddenly, my string broke!
I fell through the sky.
I was so scared! I did not know where I was going.
I closed my eyes. After some time, I stopped falling.

I opened my eyes and saw that I was hanging from the branch of a tree.
Raju climbed up a tall ladder and set me free.
He hugged me and brought me home.

THE MAGIC WATCH

One day, an old man went to the river to catch fish. Soon, he caught a fish in his net.

When the old man held the fish, it said, "Please let me go grandpa! I have a big family. They will cry for me."

The old man said, "I will not let you go. I am hungry. I will eat you for lunch."

“Please do not do that grandpa! Here, take this watch. It is a special watch. It will make all your wishes come true,” said the fish. The old man took the watch. “Hmmm! Let me see. I am keeping this.” And he put the fish back in the water.

The old man put the watch in his pocket and went home.
He forgot about his magic watch.
At night, the old man felt tired and sleepy. But it was too cold for him to sleep. He said, "How nice it would be if the Sun came out and warmed me up."

Suddenly, the sun appeared in the sky! The old man was happy! But the animals were not.

The rooster was sleeping. He rubbed his eyes and said, "I did not wake up. When did the sun rise?" He started crowing loudly. The rooster woke the birds and other animals.

The birds in the tree started chirping! The hens started clucking! The bees started buzzing. The cows started mooing loudly.

Now the old man could not sleep in the noise! He got very angry. He took the watch and threw it into the well.

Suddenly, it became night again.
The moon appeared in the sky.
It was calm and peaceful.
The animals went back to sleep.
And the old man was wide awake.